Heart Sessions with Jesus

Heart Sessions with Jesus

Basic Tools for
Healing
and Freedom

Angela Adkins

Delta River Publishing

Contents

Thank you to my dear husband, Seth Adkins, for giving me the honest feedback I needed and helping me think through each chapter and communicate more effectively. I couldn't have completed this work without you! Life is better with you in it.

Thank you to my family for believing in me and having patience with me.

Thank you Leah Fruth for the photography and for cheering me onward!

Thank you to the many dear friends who encouraged and prayed for me along the way.

Thank you to my friends from La Fuente Riviera in Puerto Vallarta, Mexico who inspired this project in the first place!

And last, but certainly not least, thank You to Father God, Holy Spirit, and Jesus for leading me and giving me the confidence to write. May this work bring glory to Your Name and help many people experience healing, freedom, and a deeper connection to You.

"He heals the broken hearted and binds up their
wounds." Psalm 147:3 (ESV)

A Letter from the Author

Dear Reader,

It is my heart's desire that you will take what is in this manual for healing, and as you apply the practical steps you will grow in leaps and bounds in your relationship with God. Almost 20 years ago, I took the first steps to heal my heart. I learned valuable lessons and began to forgive and overcome core lies that I didn't even realize were there.

I came out of a place of fear and performance based love into a place of unconditional love and acceptance which started my journey to wholeness.

As I pursued healing and freedom, I passionately shared it with everyone around me. As I learned more so did those around me. As I received healing so did they. As I unlocked my prison doors, others began to unlock their prison doors.

My hope is that I can take what has helped me in these last 20 years, and what has helped so many others along the way, and put it into a simple form that will help move you forward in your own journey of healing and freedom. The concepts are simple and powerful and will be life-changing as you put them into practice.

Even kids can learn to connect with God and use these concepts and processes. No one is too young or too old for God to heal. No one is too young or too old to hear His voice. My own children have had God speak to them at very young ages, through dreams, visions, and the Word.

If you will do the practice in these sessions and make them a part of your life, not just read the words on the page, but actually do the work with Jesus, you will see tremendous results. What I share in this workbook is not just for a one time experience with God but for a lifetime of wholeness.

Allow the anointing of Christ to heal you, the Word of God to steer you, the Holy Spirit to encounter you, and the vision of God to strengthen and encourage you. Partner with God in this process of healing your heart and you will not be disappointed.

I bless you as you step out in this adventure of discovering wholeness.
In Him,
Angela Adkins

Testimonies

"The Lord and I had done a lot of work in the forgiveness arena. I know forgiveness of others is crucial, and I always thought forgiveness was the end goal. It is not. Through this study, I learned the decision to forgive is not the end goal, rather the decision to forgive is a foundation for healing. This revelation was a game changer! Once I moved past forgiveness and onto healing from the wounds that were inflicted, I found new freedom in multiple areas of life."

\- Dawn Hauter

"I found the workbook well written and easy to understand. It helped me move closer to God."

\-Mark Rayn

"I was feeling a bit stuck in an area of my heart when I came to Angela for prayer. She was warm and kind as I sat down, but then went right to the task at hand -- to pray with me and for me for breakthrough. Her sensitivity to the Holy Spirit and her confident authority in prayer led her to pray powerfully into my situation. The result was me walking out of her office feeling lighter than when I came in and sending a stronghold had been broken.

In the coming weeks, I saw the fruit of this prayer time in some significant areas of my life! I am so grateful that Angela is walking in her gifting and authority and is being used so powerfully by God in the lives of His beloved children!"

\-Jill Ludlow

Introduction: The Purpose for Heart Sessions

The Purpose for Heart Sessions

TRAUMA AND WOUNDS OF THE HEART CAN MAKE YOU FEEL SEPARATED AND FAR AWAY FROM GOD'S LOVE. YOUR EXPERIENCE OF PAIN CAN GIVE YOU A WARPED PERSPECTIVE OF WHO GOD ACTUALLY IS, AND ALTHOUGH YOU MAY KNOW IN YOUR HEAD *ABOUT* GOD'S LOVE, IF YOU HAVE UNHEALED TRAUMA YOU MAY NOT BE FULLY ABLE TO EXPERIENCE HIS LOVE IN YOUR HEART.

The heart sessions in this workbook were created for a dual purpose:

1. To connect you to God the Father, God the Son, and God the Holy Spirit
2. To bring you into greater wholeness, restoring you to your original God-given identity.

Trauma and wounds of the heart can make you feel separated and far away from God's love. It can give you a warped perspective of who God actually is, and although you may know in your head *about* God's love, if you have unhealed trauma you may not be fully able to experience His love in your heart. While you may be walking toward His love, you likely aren't walking from a place of *being* fully loved.

These healing tools and Scriptures will help to bring a clearer perspective and remove pain from your past. All healing comes through Jesus by the Holy Spirit, and there is no other source we rely on besides Him.

Romans 12:2 says, *"And do not be conformed to this world [any longer with its superficial values and customs], but be transformed and progressively changed [as you mature spiritually] by the renewing of your mind [focusing on godly values and ethical attitudes], so that you may prove [for yourselves] what the will of God is, that which is good and acceptable and perfect [in His plan and purpose for you]."* (AMP)

When we moved into our house in Bradenton, FL in 2010, it needed work to make it a home. The water in the pool was black and murky, there was a huge gaping hole in one of the walls, mold in some of the bathrooms, old carpet and paint that needed refreshing. It was so bad that my husband actually lived there for a month without us to repair it and make it ready for us to live in. The stairs were all different heights and they were a danger zone for tripping.

When we left that house 8 years later, we had replaced the entire stairway and painstakingly hand-stained each of the new treads, making them even like they should have been in the first place. The finished result was beautiful. The bathrooms were redone, the plumbing had been overhauled, the walls repaired and new paint and flooring put in. Even the closets had been redone. The pool was clear and had been used for swimming, and many memories had been created in that house over those years.

The house still wasn't perfect when we moved, there were some areas outside that needed new support, and the kitchen we later found out had mold in the walls. What we couldn't see we didn't know about. Anyone that has owned a house knows it takes constant care and upkeep to create a great home environment.

It also takes constant care and upkeep to create a great heart environment.

If we look at our minds and hearts as a place that needs renewal and care and a home for the Holy Spirit (ref. I Corinthians 6:19) to dwell in, we will be more apt to accept and embrace the change we need. It's hard to get rid of the old if we don't see the purpose for it. But when we can see the new and how much better it will be, then letting go of the old stinkin' thinkin' becomes much easier.

There are places in our hearts and lives that need repair, and some places that need fresh revelation like fresh paint is to a home, and some things that need to be completely removed and replaced. When a house is renovated specific tools and skill sets are used to accomplish the plans, and it is no different to renew your mind and restore and repair your heart. It takes tools from the Holy Spirit to renovate your mind. We are encouraged in Romans 12:2 to be transformed and progressively changed by renewing our minds. Just as a home is in constant need of cleaning or repair, our hearts and minds need continual renewal, tearing down old lies and faulty foundations and rebuilding new thought patterns with truth.

The intent of these sessions with God is to restore communion and intimacy between God and you. This is done by exposing and removing the lies of the enemy and receiving God's truth over you so you can be fully healed from the past and able to flourish in the future God has for you. Your past does not define you or your future. God doesn't want you stuck in your past, your sin, or your pain.

There are many principles that can be used to help you on your journey of personal healing, and helping others heal. We are going to unwrap a few of these together in *Heart Sessions with Jesus Volume 1.*
The goal of the following sessions is to:

1. Bring healing to your own heart
2. Help you know how to bring healing to others.

The way this booklet is set up is so that you can go through a session, learn how to use the principle, the why behind it, and then apply and experience it in your own life. When a handyman pulls tools out of a workbench, they do him no good if he doesn't know how to use them. A hammer isn't a screwdriver, and a screwdriver isn't a drill. A handyman's tools become much more valuable when he knows when and how to use them. Using a screwdriver to hang a picture isn't going to work, but grab the hammer instead and the picture is up in a moment, ready to be admired by anyone who comes by. In the same way, knowing about principles for healing isn't the same as knowing how to use the principles correctly.

The purpose of the following heart sessions is for you to learn the principles and concepts, and then be able to practically put into practice what you have learned to bring healing and renovation to your own heart. Be gracious to yourself as you learn how to apply what you learn in this workbook to your own life and heart.

Once you have applied the concept and have seen the benefits for yourself, you will be able to help others apply them as well.

Heart Session: Created for Relationship

Created for Relationship

God created you for a relationship with Him and with others. In Genesis 3:8, God walked with Adam and Eve in the cool of the day because He wanted to be in a relationship with them. When sin entered the scene, the perfect relationship as they knew it was broken. In a perfect relationship there is no hiding. Adam and Eve hid and tried to cover themselves from God after they sinned. Just like Adam and Eve, we have a gut nature of hiding and shame when we miss the mark, when we fail. We fall short. Our sin brings about death and death means no relationship or intimacy with the Father. Romans 3:23 says, *"for we all have sinned and fall short of the glory of God"* (ESV)

If you haven't experienced this type of relationship with God you may wonder why it is so important. Intimacy with Father God wakes you up to who you are and your true identity. This is why He sent Jesus. Jesus came to repair the gap between us and the Father, to give us life and make a way back to His heart.

Romans 3:24 explains this further, *"(all) are justified by his grace as a gift, through the redemption that is in Christ Jesus, whom God put forward as a propitiation (atonement and reconciliation) by his blood, to be received by faith."* (ESV)

The bad news is sin causes pain, hiding, and shame in our worlds.

The good news is that Jesus heals and liberates us from all of our sin!

"I am the Way, the Truth, and the Life. No one comes to My Father except through me." John 14:6 (NKJV) Jesus is the bridge, the one that redeems.

It is really important to note that every healing principle that is shared on this journey is meant to bring us back into connection and relationship with Jesus, Holy Spirit, and the Father. All healing comes through the Godhead. All freedom comes through the Godhead. There is no other way of healing. This may sound uncompromising, but when we take any other route we are only prolonging the pain and the lies we are living in.

In the beginning God created all things and science is the discovery of how God masterfully wove all those things together. God did not just make us with reason and logic, but also with creativity and imagination. Sometimes, we can rely too heavily on reasoning and logic and miss what God wants to speak to us in our spirit. Colossians 3:2 says, *"Set your mind and keep focused habitually on the things above [the heavenly things], not on things that are on earth [which only have temporal value]."* (AMP) God created us with the ability to perceive, see, and understand not only physical things but spiritual things. Our imagination can be a platform God uses to show us truth and bring us healing.

Paul says in Ephesians 1:17, *"[I always pray] that the God of our Lord Jesus Christ, the Father of glory, may grant you a spirit of wisdom and of revelation [that gives you deep and personal and intimate insight] into the true knowledge of Him [for we know the Father through the Son]. And [I pray] that the eyes of your heart [the very center and core of your being] may be enlightened [flooded with light by the Holy Spirit], so that you will know and cherish the hope [the divine guarantee, the confident expectation] to which He has called you, the riches of His glorious inheritance in the saints, and [so that you will begin to know] what the immeasurable and unlimited and surpassing greatness of His [active spiritual] power is in us who believe."* (AMP)

II Corinthians 4:4 talks about how the god of this world has blinded the minds of the unbelieving. *"...the god of this world [Satan] has blinded the minds of the unbelieving to prevent them from seeing the illuminating light of the gospel of the glory of Christ, who is the image of God."* (AMP) The enemy does not want you or I to see spiritually or to use our imagination for the things and thoughts of the Lord. He wants us blinded so we can't receive healing or truth that restores. God wants us to be enlightened and see what He sees so we can be healed, sound of mind, and free from lies.

God doesn't want us to have a flat approach to Him, but rather, to have a full experience with Him. He made us body, soul, and spirit, and wants us engaged with Him and His plan in a full body, soul, and spirit experience. He wants you to know how to love Him with all your heart, soul, mind, and strength(body). (ref. Mark 12:30)

We often limit Him to just one part of our lives or a certain level of experience. Ultimately, as you go through *Heart Sessions with Jesus* the goal is to have no room closed off or untouched by the Spirit of God, to walk in full surrender and full renewal in every area including our emotions and our mind. Often as we are healed and renewed in our hearts and minds, we will begin to experience physical healing as well. What happens internally also affects us externally.

Keep in mind how open and honest you are with yourself and Jesus as you go through these sessions will directly correlate to how much value you receive from the sessions.

Let's Practice

Take a minute and offer your mind, your heart, and your body to the Lord. Let Him know that you are surrendering your thoughts and your emotions, and even your physical pain to Him and that you don't want to hold anything back.

Ask Him if there has been anything specific that you have been withholding from Him.

If so, Why? Are you afraid? What are you afraid of?

Do you need to be in control? Why?

Do you trust Jesus? Why or why not?

Delve in deeper to the places that could hold you back in the following practices and applications. Now is the time to surrender the control to Jesus and let go of the fear and anything else that could hold you back from your healing.

Write down what He shows you or speaks to you:

2

Heart Session: Connecting with Jesus

Connecting with Jesus

"I will take my stand at my watch-post and station myself on the tower, and look out to see what he will say to me, and what I will answer concerning my complaint. And the Lord answered me, Write the vision, make it plain on tablets, so he may run who reads it. For still the vision awaits its appointed time; it hastens to the end—it will not lie. If it seems slow, wait for it; it will surely come; it will not delay."(Habakkuk 2:1-3) (ESV)

Habakkuk 2:1-3 has changed my world as I receive from God for myself and minister to others. Note that it says *"Look out to see what he will say to me."* We are to look to see what God will say, not just listen to hear what He will say. This means we position ourselves to use our the eyes of our hearts as we communicate with the Lord. I first learned about this when I took *Communion with God,* a college course that was offered at the church I attended in Florida.

From this basis in Habbakuk, and many other Scriptures about dreams, vision, and imaginations, we see the Lord desires that we use all our senses to receive His messages to us including using our sight. What Habakkuk received was from prophetic revelation through spiritual vision. He looked to see what God would say.

We were created to use all our senses for God, but when we use them for the wrong things we can end up dull to the things of the Spirit. When we don't use our sight at all, it's like a muscle that doesn't get used, and it becomes weak and useless.

In this session, you will start exercising the muscle of sight and letting God speak through it to you. Part of hearing God is looking to see what He will say. As we open our heart and mind to hear from God, we need to make sure obstacles are removed. I cover how to overcome obstacles in our connection with God in more depth with our *Heart Sessions with Jesus Volume 2.*

For now, let's look at a few obstacles mentioned in II Corinthians 10:4-6.

"For although we live in the natural realm, we don't wage a military campaign employing human weapons, using manipulation to achieve our aims. Instead, our spiritual weapons are energized with divine power to effectively dismantle the defenses behind which people hide. We can demolish every deceptive fantasy that opposes God and break through every arrogant attitude that is raised up in defiance of the true knowledge of God. We capture, like prisoners of war, every thought and insist that it bows in obedience to the Anointed One. Since we are armed with such dynamic weaponry, we stand ready to punish any trace of rebellion, as soon as we choose complete obedience." II Corinthians 10:4-6 (TPT)

The obstacles mentioned in this Scripture are as follows: defenses behind which we hide, deceptive fantasies, arrogant attitudes, and disobedient thoughts. A huge part of healing and freedom is to dismantle what the enemy has built in our lives and establish truth. So let's look in a little more depth at these four obstacles.

Defenses behind which we hide: In the same way that Adam and Eve hid in the garden after they sinned, we can hold on to our sin and cover ourselves. Jesus made it so we don't have to hide anymore, He paid the price for our sin, but He won't heal things we are hiding from Him. In Mark 3, Jesus called the man with the withered hand to Himself, and then asked him to stretch out his hand. Not the good hand, but the withered hand. When the man stretched out his withered hand, Jesus healed it.

Even more uncomfortable than uncovering our pain, part of the healing process is also confessing our own sin to others.

James 1:5 says, "Confess your sins one to another and pray for one another, and you will be healed." Genuine real confession brings healing. We have to be willing to come out of our hiding place and get real with Jesus and others.

Deceptive fantasies: "For the time is coming when they will no longer listen and respond to the healing words of truth because they will become selfish and proud. They will seek out teachers with soothing words that line up with their desires, saying just what they want to hear. They will close their ears to the truth and believe nothing but fables and myths. So be alert to all these things and overcome every form of evil." II Timothy 3:3-4 (TPT)

True healing doesn't come by hearing the words we want to hear, it comes by hearing the words we need to hear. If we are looking to be comforted in our sin, rather than rescued from it, then we won't receive healing words of truth. Everything you hear and see from Jesus in your vision and imagination needs to line up with the truth of the Word of God. There are many lies in our culture that lead to fantasy rather than genuine healing. Spirit guides, crystals, self-empowerment, independence from God; these are just a few of the things that can look appealing but are deceptive fantasies. Deceptive fantasies are hard to spot because they appeal to us, and the seeds can be sown through spiritual authority as well, which is why we need to be discerning in what we receive.

Arrogant Attitudes: If we think we know more than we do, or are not open for God to reveal our hearts and teach us, we won't receive breakthrough.
"God resists the proud, but gives grace to the humble." James 4:6 (ESV)
If we think we know more than God, He won't show us what we don't know. If we position ourselves to willingly receive from God and to be open and teachable, breakthrough, healing, and freedom can be experienced.

Disobedient thoughts: Other versions of Scripture say impure imaginations in place of disobedient thoughts. These type of thoughts keep us from the true knowledge of God and keep us captive. These thoughts come in many different forms, such as impure, perverse thoughts; lies about ourselves. Gossip, slander, and rebellion are all in the realm of thoughts of disobedience. If we don't take our thoughts and desires captive, James 1:13-15 explains further that our desires (thoughts) give birth to sin and sin brings forth death.
"Let no one say when he is tempted, "I am being tempted by God," for God cannot be tempted with evil, and He Himself tempts no one. But each person is tempted when he is lured and enticed by his own desire. then desire when it has conceived gives birth to sin, and sin when it is fully grown brings forth death." James 1:13-15 (ESV)

If you embrace the truth, it will release true freedom into your lives.

As you connect with Jesus, look for what He is saying to you, and choose to trust Him. If you see any of these four obstacles in your thought life, bring them to Him.

When I first meet with people and we practice this concept of connecting with Jesus, I ask them to use the eyes of their heart and go to a peaceful place. Many people end up picturing the beach or a body of water or find themselves imagining something out in nature. God's creation brings us peace. Other times the place that brings them peace might be a bedroom or a clean empty room with a couch, or somewhere where they feel safe.

Surgeons don't do surgery in the middle of chaos if they can help it. They provide a clean, sterile environment that is safe from germs and distractions that can take away the success of the surgery. In the same way, when you invite Jesus to heal your heart, it's much easier if you can find a space that is away from distractions and is safe where you can let your guard down.

We need to be connected to Jesus because He is the source of life.

In John 15:4-5, Jesus says, *"Abide in me, and I in you. As the branch cannot bear fruit by itself, unless it abides in the vine, neither can you, unless you abide in me. I am the vine; you are the branches. Whoever abides in me and I in him, he it is that bears much fruit, for apart from me you can do nothing."(ESV)* As you live with Jesus as your source, there will be fruitfulness- but when you live separated from Jesus you are powerless.

The whole point of practicing connection with Jesus is so we can have a power-filled life that bears good fruit and is full of love and obedience.

Before you step into the practice below, find a place where you can be quiet and undistracted as much as possible. Put away and silence your phone. Take a notebook to write down any important thoughts that might come and distract you. This will clear your mind and give you peace to listen.

Once you settle in, then it's time to wait and see what God will say to you.

Let's Practice

Read John 15: 1-17 and meditate on it.

Jesus knows how each one of us connects, and He can speak our language.

Ask the Lord if you have used your vision for things you shouldn't have. Pornography, impure movies, witchcraft/occult involvement are a few things that can block your vision and hinder you from receiving.

Confess anything the Holy Spirit brings to mind, break agreement with those sins and thought patterns, and ask the Lord to restore your sight. Confess any of the four obstacles (defenses behind which we hide, deceptive fantasies, arrogant attitudes, disobedient thoughts) you may have related to in this session. Find someone you can trust and confess the sin to them.

Once you have prepared yourself, ask the question: Where is a place you love to go that brings you peace and comfort?
Find that safe space with God. Practice using your vision to see what God wants to say. Close your eyes, get relaxed and clear out all distractions. If a distracting thought comes to mind and won't go away, write it down for later so it doesn't interrupt the process. Ask the Lord to join you. Once He has joined you, let Him take the lead in what He wants to show you.

Ask Jesus this question: Lord, what do you want to show me and say to me?

Write down what you see, hear, and experience (this can come in the form of vision, a flow of words, and even emotions from within, look with the eyes of your heart.)

You can also write anything He shows you from the John 15 reading as well.

3

Heart Session: Inviting Jesus into Memories

Inviting Jesus into Memories

> JESUS CHRIST IS THE SAME YESTERDAY AND TODAY AND FOREVER. HE IS ABLE TO HEAL US AT ANY POINT OF OUR EXPERIENCE AND IS NOT LIMITED BY TIME OR SPACE.

In this session we are going to discuss what it looks like to go on a journey with Jesus. One of the most beautiful things about His love and ministry to us is that He takes broken things and makes them whole. To do that we have to go into the broken places with Him and allow Him to reveal what made them broken in the first place. What He reveals He chooses to heal. What I mean by this is that when we submit ourselves and we give the eyes of our heart to the Lord and we ask Him to speak to us, sometimes He will take us into an experience in the past where it adjusted our belief system. That adjustment gives power to lies and thought patterns that lead us on a path that takes us away from who God created us to be.

An example of a time that this happened for me was when I was dealing with fear, and the Lord showed me a box in this room that I needed to get rid of (I was seeing this picture with the eyes of my heart). When I went to remove the box, it disappeared like a mirage and then would reappear when I stepped back. As I processed this with another person who was ministering to me, she suggested that perhaps the box represented worry in my life. Something that was there but wasn't really existent. That made a lot of sense, so I asked the Lord where the worry came in. He brought me to a memory of when I was three or four years of age. I would have never thought of it without the Holy Spirit's help.

My dad, coming out of the hippy era and into the 80s, unbeknownst to my mom and I, had decided to cut his longish mousy blonde hair and shave his shaggy beard. In the memory the Lord showed me I was sitting and watching her get ready. My dad walked into the house and back to where we were. I was shocked as I saw him and did not recognize him as my dad. I remember thinking, "how did a stranger get into our house?" My safe zone had suddenly become threatened. My mom also looked shocked as she had no idea my dad was going to cut his hair. Then, he did the unthinkable. He kissed my mom. My mom was too busy dealing with her own shock to see the fear that I was experiencing not knowing it was my dad kissing her.

In this memory, Jesus showed me He was beside me, and He came over and reassured my little three/four year old self, "It's going to be ok." The worry lifted. What my mom had been unable to do because of her own shock from my dad's haircut, Jesus did with just a few words of assurance. It was all I needed. I forgave my parents and repented for letting worry control me.

Later, after sharing that memory with my mom and how worry had rooted itself in my life at that point, she reflected on those years. She told me that around that age I changed from a rather bossy confident kid into a more worried, hide behind her skirts kind of child. I remember especially when grown men or teenage boys would come around that I didn't know, I would hide behind her or run out of the room. All my life into my twenties I dealt with intimidation especially with men I didn't know well. As I received healing and recognized the seeds of worry that were planted from that simple situation as a child, I began to overcome worry and intimidation and step out in more areas, especially leadership. Worry had been rooted in such a simple memory, totally unfounded, but yet it had crept in and grabbed me. The Holy Spirit knew exactly where to take me to get to the root of my worry, and speak truth to it. The truth was simple. I was going to be ok. I was safe.

When you move into the practice and Jesus brings a memory to you, present the memory back to Jesus and ask Him what is it about what He is showing you that He wants to speak into. At times, He will bring up a series of memories that all relate to one another. If no memory comes up, you can directly ask Him if there are any memories he would like to heal and speak truth into. You don't have to force this to happen, and if there are no current memories that come to mind for you, you can tuck this in your tool belt for someday when you need it. Inviting Jesus into memories works, whether we bring the memory to Him or He brings it to us, the result of healing is the same.

When a memory is brought up, don't put yourself back in the memory. Look at the memory like you are looking through a window, and watch the memory with Jesus. The reason I encourage this is because it isn't always best to relive a memory, especially when it is a traumatic memory. It's better to view it as an outsider looking in. Jesus never brings up a memory to create more trauma, but rather, to give a new perspective and heal the trauma that happened in that moment.

In some cases we will bring something up to Jesus where He won't answer, or He will show us something completely different. As we are not manufacturing these experiences, but letting the Holy Spirit lead, we are not in control of what's happening. Allowing Jesus to minister into whatever He wants to show us or wherever He wants to go is ideal because what He reveals He heals. He sees a bigger picture and knows what we need.

Some ways to invite Jesus to speak into a memory is through these questions:

"Jesus, where were you when this happened? What do you want to show me about this memory? What truth do you want to speak to me?"

At this point, you wait in faith for the Lord to show you where He is and what He wants to say or do. Sometimes it's as simple as a hug and letting you know you are ok like in my situation above. Sometimes He speaks the truth of the Word where we believed a lie. Sometimes He shows us how to love ourselves where we have experienced rejection. There can be so many things He wants to show us and speak to us, every situation will be unique. Be open and don't limit what Jesus can do.

Recently, I had a friend revisit a memory Jesus had already healed. She asked the Lord why He had brought her back to the same memory she had already received healing in. She could have shut the picture down because she had already been there, but instead, she asked Jesus where He was in the memory and what He wanted to show her. She didn't make any premature assumptions and let Him lead.

This time, rather than showing her He was by her side in the memory (which was what happened the first time she saw the picture with Jesus), He showed her He was sitting with her sister and playing. She had always felt guilt as the older sister that she wasn't enough for her little sister. Jesus was showing her that He was there with her sister the whole time as well. She wasn't responsible for her sister's life's decisions and didn't need to be ashamed or feel she wasn't enough. The first time Jesus showed her the memory He was bringing her healing from the personal trauma she had experienced in her childhood home. The second time He showed her the memory, He was taking away shame and false guilt that she hadn't been enough for her sister and showing her that He was also with the rest of the family through this difficult time. He used the same memory to bring further healing to her perspective and her heart, and she was freed from a sense of false responsibility because she didn't limit Him.

This is a beautiful example of not putting an expectation on Jesus but letting him show us what he wants to show us. He knows us better than we know ourselves, and he knows at what point we accepted a lie about our identity or had a shattering experience. He isn't just Lord of our present, but also our future and our past. *"Jesus Christ is the same yesterday and today and forever."* Hebrews 13:8 (ESV) He is able to heal us at any point of our experience and is not limited by time or space.

Another time, I was leading someone through a session that had been through some intense trauma and abuse as a young child. I expected God to bring her back to that memory and bring healing to it, but instead he showed her a memory of herself and her grandma that was peaceful and wonderful. Through that He helped her see she needed to forgive the other family member that had hurt her and then Jesus gave her a gift of peace. He brought her to a place in her child-hood that represented peace, rather than cause her to go back to the painful memory of abuse.

Be careful not to assume how the Lord is going to heal. He knows exactly what we need for our heart to heal. The beautiful part about these sessions is that we are partnering with the Holy Spirit and letting Him lead us into healing. What may bring healing for one person may not be the same for another because we are each unique and our experiences in life are unique.

We are never beyond healing. As a minister, my husband has helped a lot of people receive freedom and healing through Jesus. At one of the conferences he was at years ago, as he was preparing to teach on healing, the Holy Spirit unblocked a memory for him personally. A painful memory he hadn't even remembered up to that point. He ended up hiding in a closet in the middle of the conference, unsure what he should do and just wanting to run away. Here he was supposed to be teaching about healing, and he was just brought face to face with an extremely broken and traumatic moment in his own life. Our senior leader found him in the closet, and he used the tool of inviting Jesus into the memory. Through that experience Jesus healed his trauma, and helped my husband renew his mind and establish a new core belief where the trauma had been.

I wanted to share his story because it isn't unusual for someone with deep trauma, sexual trauma, or physical abuse to have blocked memories due to the level of trauma. Trust the Lord when He opens up something of this nature, He is wanting to heal it and He is safe. Don't be afraid of Jesus revealing something that has been covered or forgotten in your life. What He reveals, He heals. Jesus never shows us things to cause more pain in our lives. Sometimes we have to walk through the discomfort of the trauma to get us to the other side, but Jesus' ultimate goal is always healing, restoration, and freedom.

It's important to share with someone when an experience like this happens. When you confess to someone else what has happened, whether it is something you have done, or something that was done to you, there is freedom in the confession, and a promise from the Lord that you will be healed. *"Confess your sins one to another and pray for one another, and you will be healed."* (James 5:16 ESV) Even if it is the sin of another that was done unto you, confession and forgiveness are a huge part of the process of healing from that wound.

If you are brought to a place that is too painful to deal with alone, I highly encourage you to bring your experience to someone who is trained in healing trauma to help you walk through it. You can schedule a session at angelaadkins.com if you don't know where else to go.

Let's Practice

Go to your safe space with the Lord, the place you have already established with Him. Once He is there with you, ask Jesus if He would like to reveal a memory to you that needs healing. Or, perhaps an experience already came up during the practice you did previously, and now you can dive further into that.

Once Jesus shows you a memory, ask Jesus "Where are you in this memory? What do you want to show me? What do you want to heal?"

--

When Jesus answers you, continue to ask Him,
"Lord, is there anything else you want to say to me or show me?"

--

Stay in the experience with Him until it is over.
Once the experience is over, write it down so you don't forget. Let the Lord continue to speak truth to you about the situation. Feel free to ask Him questions and let Him lead you to truth and healing.

{ 4 }

Heart Session: Forgiveness is a Foundation

Forgiveness is a Foundation

I CAN IMAGINE PETER SQUIRMING IN HIS SEAT. THIS MEANS HE CAN'T *EVER* HOLD A GRUDGE. EVEN THE ANNOYING FISHERMAN WHO ALWAYS STOLE THE PRIZE SPOT FISHING– THAT GUY HAD TO BE FORGIVEN TOO.

My favorite story about forgiveness is found in the Bible in Matthew 18.

Peter comes to Jesus and asks Him, "How many times do I have to forgive? Seven times?" I have to laugh at this because Peter has to be thinking religiously— *seven is a good Christian number. The number of wholeness and perfection. If I am willing to forgive a person seven times, that has to be holy, and then surely I have done my duty.*

However, Jesus answers him, "Peter, not seven times, but seventy times seven."

Perfection isn't enough Peter– it's perfect times perfect. Forgive until you are made perfect, and then keep forgiving.

I can imagine Peter squirming in his seat. This means he can't *ever* hold a grudge. Even the annoying fisherman who always stole the prize spot fishing– that guy had to be forgiven too. And the tax collector that overcharged him every year. And that judgmental Pharisee that looked down on him every time they crossed paths because he had gotten better grades in Torah school. They all had to be forgiven.

Jesus goes on to tell, in my opinion, one of the most powerful stories in Scripture. There was a man who owed a ruler a lot of money, millions of dollars, and he was called to account by the king of the land. The man begged for mercy, and miraculously the king had compassion on him and forgave him the debt completely. You would think the man would have gone home kissing and forgiving everyone around him because the ruler had saved him from prison and given him a new life with no debt. What did this man do instead? He went home and on the way home, he met a servant of his who owed him a smaller amount of money. He demanded this man pay up. The servant he met on the road begs the man who was forgiven his debt for mercy. Sound familiar? Wasn't this man just doing the same thing a day ago? But instead of forgiving the servant who owed him money, the man has him hauled off to prison and says, "Pay up buddy."

Word gets back to the king of how the man had treated his servant. He calls him back into court, furious. "Is this the way you respond to my mercy?! Because you begged me, I forgave the massive debt you owed me. Why didn't you show the same mercy to your fellow servant that I showed to you?" And the king turned him over to prison guards to be tortured until all his debt was repaid. Then, at the end of the story, Jesus says the most sobering thing. "In this same way, my heavenly Father will deal with any of you if you do not release forgiveness from your heart toward your fellow believer."

Forgiveness literally releases us out of a prison sentence. Un-forgiveness puts us in bondage, plain and simple, just like the man in the story. Isaiah 61 says of Jesus, "the Lord has anointed me...to proclaim liberty to the captives and the opening of the prison to those who are bound." This is referring to the act Jesus did on the cross releasing forgiveness to us, and we are then responsible to live from the foundation of forgiveness. The story Jesus told is an example of what we experience through Christ's mercy. We are forgiven by God, and then we are supposed to go out and show mercy to those around us.

But what do we often do to those that have hurt us deeply or owe us something? We say, "Pay up buddy, or I will make you pay! There is no way I am forgiving you for this."
This response literally breaks God's heart and makes Him angry with us, and puts us in a prison of our own making when we could be free.

We make a choice every day to live in our pain when we choose not to forgive. Jesus made a way for us to be forgiven for eternity, and yet, many times, we don't have the mercy to turn around and do the same for others. We are forgiven by Christ, but if we choose not to forgive, God actually gives permission for us to be tormented mentally, physically, and emotionally until we are able to forgive, release the offense and show mercy to those around us. This is one way that the devil has legal entrance into our lives. He is permitted to stay and wreak havoc when we harbor bitterness or un-forgiveness in our hearts. We cannot be free until we forgive.

Forgiveness is a command from Christ. It isn't optional. It's not only for those that deserve it. In fact that is the point of forgiveness. No one deserves it. Romans 6:23 says the wages of sin is death. We all deserve death, not forgiveness. Yet Christ forgave us.

One of the things a mentor of mine taught me is that "Forgiveness is *not* an emotion, it is a choice!" I will always hear her voice speaking that out in my head. Now other people hear my voice in their head saying that phrase. I will never stop saying it because it's true, and when we choose to forgive, it's powerful and it's freeing. If we wait until we *feel* like forgiving, we will never forgive. No one feels like forgiving ever, because what people do to us hurts. Our flesh wants them to pay for the pain they have caused. But we don't live by that flesh. According to Romans 8:13 *"when you live controlled by the flesh, you are about to die. But if the life of the Spirit puts to death the corrupt ways of the flesh, we THEN taste his abundant life!!!"*

Forgiveness is the foundation for our healing and freedom. It will release us from our prison and our pain. One time, a lady came up for prayer ministry and her request was for healing. She had severe pain in her back and told me it was caused by arthritis. I remembered someone telling me once that arthritis can be caused by un-forgiveness, so I asked the lady if there was anyone she needed to forgive and explained to her that her forgiveness would be the doorway to her healing. She didn't hesitate and said yes she had someone to forgive. Immediately I led her through forgiveness and then commanded healing over her back. Her face told it all. Shocked, she said, "The pain left."

I am not saying all arthritis is due to un-forgiveness or bitterness, but I am saying that our bitterness can cause physical pain and ailments.

Personally, I have found that when I forgive people and refuse to be offended, I am less affected emotionally by others choices and I can't be controlled negatively by other people. But when I get trapped in offense, I then find myself on a roller-coaster of emotions and unstable in a lot of ways, controlled by what others think of me or want of me, and constantly feeling hurt and rejected.

Rejection can be real, but rejection doesn't have to control us. When we walk in mercy and forgiveness, we are able to recognize our own value and that it doesn't rely on what others think or do. We are also able to more easily forgive ourselves and receive Christ's forgiveness.

Let's Practice

Mark 11:25-26: *"And whenever you stand praying, if you find that you carry something in your heart against another person, release him and forgive him so that your Father in heaven will also release you and forgive you of your faults. But if you will not release forgiveness, don't expect your Father in heaven to release you from your misdeeds."*

Take some time and read Matthew 18:21-25 for yourself.

Once you have read the passage and reflected, take some time with Jesus. If you want to go with the eyes of your heart to a safe place with Him and talk that's great, if you just want to close your eyes and picture Jesus in front of you that is fine too. The important thing is to do this with Jesus.

If you had a person or multiple people come up in the previous sessions through a memory or as you were connecting with Jesus, ask yourself if you have forgiven them. If they caused any pain in your life, they are worth taking the time to forgive. Don't skirt past it because it doesn't seem important and don't excuse their behavior as too minimal to forgive either. Nothing is too small or too big to forgive. Leave no rock behind. Overturn every place that could possibly be harboring bitterness or offense in your heart, and choose forgiveness.

Ask Jesus who you need to forgive. Make a list below of the people you need to forgive and why. The list may come from previous sessions, or it can be a completely new list. Don't excuse people for their behaviors, forgiveness isn't making it less or excusing it. It's releasing the offense and the offender and not harboring bitterness in your heart.

Pray this prayer of forgiveness over each person:

Lord, I *choose* to forgive ____________________ for ________________________________. I forgive him/her completely and totally and release him/her to You. I release any anger, bitterness, pain, jealousy, (fill in the emotions you are having) ____________________ to you and ask that you would take it all.

Pray this prayer over each of the persons on your list. As you pray, picture yourself giving Jesus that person and the pain that has come with the situation. If you were abandoned by your mother or father, give Him that abandonment. If fear came in through a situation, forgive the person who caused the fear, and then give the fear over to Jesus.

Then picture Jesus taking these things out of your heart. Bitterness, anger, rejection, pain, even physical ailments, they are all real experiences and emotions that we have, and when we forgive we also need to release all of those things to Jesus. He delivers us from our tormenters when we forgive. All of these things are tormentors.

Write about what the Lord is showing you through this process:

____

____

____

____

____

As I shared previously, I have seen people healed from back pain and arthritis when they forgive. I have seen people delivered from demons after they forgive. I have seen internal sicknesses disappear after people forgive. I have seen mental illnesses overcome through forgiveness and a release of control.

I challenge you to make this practice of forgiveness a daily routine in your life. When you feel offense trying to creep in, choose not to be offended and immediately forgive the person. Ask the Lord if there are any personal adjustments to make, and move forward. One time, when I was upset with Seth (my husband), I remember refusing to go to bed angry, and I stayed up on the couch til 2am saying over and over "I choose to forgive Seth for __________." I said it until I meant it. It took a few hours before I felt my heart fully release the anger and agree with the words I was saying, but the next morning, I was able to walk in love toward him again. To be honest, to this day, I can't even remember what I was offended about. I just remember the hours it took to forgive him. It's worth it to forgive.

Remember, if you want to be shown mercy, then walk showing mercy to others.

{ 5 }

Heart Session: The Divine Exchange

The Divine Exchange

YOU WERE WORTH HIM GOING TO THE CROSS, SURELY YOU ARE WORTH HIM GIVING YOU WHAT YOU NEED. ISAIAH 61:3 SAYS HE GIVES BEAUTY FOR ASHES, AND JOY FOR MOURNING. IT'S A DIVINE EXCHANGE. IT'S YOUR COAL FOR HIS DIAMOND, IT'S YOUR DIRT FOR HIS REDEMPTION.

"The Spirit of the Lord God is upon me, because the Lord has anointed me to bring good news to the poor; he has sent me to bind up the brokenhearted, to proclaim liberty to the captives, and the opening of the prison to those who are bound; to proclaim the year of the Lord's favor, and the day of vengeance of our God; to comfort all who mourn; to grant to those who mourn in Zion-- to give them a beautiful headdress instead of ashes, the oil of gladness instead of mourning, the garment of praise instead of a faint spirit; that they may be called oaks of righteousness, the planting of the Lord, that he may be glorified. They shall build up the ancient ruins; they shall raise up the former devastations; they shall repair the ruined cities, the devastations of many generations…instead of shame there will be a double portion; instead of dishonor they shall rejoice in their lot; therefore in their land they shall possess a double portion; they shall have everlasting joy." (Isaiah 61:1-4,7) (ESV)

Isaiah 61:1-4,7 shows an exchange that God gives us something wonderful when we give Him our ugliness. For example, perhaps someone releases their bitterness, and He gives them healing from arthritis. Perhaps someone has been in mourning and He gives them gladness and joy. Perhaps someone is weary, discouraged, and hopeless, and He gives them praise, joy, and strength in return. This is how our amazing God works. He takes our pain and sin and returns to us healing, freedom, and the overcoming power that we need.

Once you have given over to Jesus the things you have been holding on to (the act of forgiveness), and have asked Jesus to take your pain, your abandonment, your bitterness, fear, anger, rejection, or whatever else He showed you to give Him, as mentioned in the previous session, go back to the picture/vision where you gave all that to Him. Look at Jesus again and ask Him:

"Now that I have forgiven and given you this _______________ (fill in the blank), what would you like to give to me in return?"

For whatever reason, asking Jesus what He wants to give in exchange for the junk we give Him can be the hardest part for us to do. Forgiving yourself and receiving a gift from Him means that you have value. If it is hard to receive a gift or blessing from Jesus, ask Him why. Get to the bottom of the lie you are believing, and let Him replace it with truth.

Receiving is a huge part of our healing. Receiving is a needed part of life. There are reasons why our receivers get broken or shut down. Maybe expectations weren't met by parents, maybe a sibling broke trust when they were needed, maybe we were taught not to rely on anyone else. Culture can teach subliminally that it isn't ok to receive, or that we don't matter enough, that we aren't valuable. Sometimes it isn't easy to receive because defenses are up so the pain can't come in, but in reality, the walls keeping the pain out also are keeping the good things out.

If your receiver is broken, take the time to work through that with the Lord. Jesus did what He saw His Father doing. He received and then He gave. When you receive love from God, you are able to give it away. When you receive, you have more to give. It's a mindset. Rarely a morning goes by without me speaking to Holy Spirit.

"Good morning, Holy Spirit, what do you have to show me or speak to me today?"

I make it a habit of receiving from Him. Receiving what Jesus did on the cross. Receiving healing, receiving freedom, receiving love. I even receive correction. When I take the time to receive then I am a much nicer person, I am a more well-adjusted person, and I am made whole by what I receive from God. Whole people are people who know how to receive and give, not just one or the other. If you look through the Bible, the people Jesus made whole received from Him, and many of them joined Him in His ministry afterward. If you were worth Him going to the cross, surely you are worth Him giving you what you need. Isaiah 61:3 says He gives beauty for ashes, and joy for mourning. It's a divine exchange. It's your coal for His diamond, it's your dirt for His redemption.

One of my favorite personal experiences of receiving from Jesus was in Mexico. I was asked to come and do some training with some leaders of a church in Puerto Vallarta and we stayed with some dear friends of ours there. When I arrived I had no gas in my tank. I was absolutely exhausted and on the verge of tears. We had been through a tough and draining season of ministry, and with our six kids at home and a new job, it seemed like I never got a break. When I got to Mexico I felt like I was closer to a mental breakdown than prepared to do a week of intense ministry training. The friends we stayed with had a condo with a pool and when we arrived, they graciously asked us what we wanted to do for the few hours we had before our meetings started. I was peopled out, and while I didn't want to be offensive, all I wanted was to go to the pool and have a couple hours where I could soak in the sun and be away from people. Our friends were so gracious and completely understood and off I went to the sunshine.

As soon as I laid on my towel and turned my attention to the Lord, He was there. I cried out, "Lord how am I supposed to do this? I am on empty and I have nothing to give." Immediately I felt His Presence pouring into me. "I love you daughter and I am so proud of you." I began to sob. I hadn't even done anything yet, how could He be proud of me? And yet He was. He began to fill me with love, with strength, with energy. By the time that hour or two by the pool was over, I felt like a new person. Sure, the sun was wonderful, but it wasn't the sun that changed the state of being, it was receiving His love for me. He was proud of me even before I trained people, even before I did "stuff" for Him. All I had to give Him was exhaustion and tears on the verge of mental breakdown, and He gave me strength, affirmation, and mental stability.

Let's Practice

Meditate on Isaiah 61:1-4, 7

Open your heart to hear from the Lord. When Jesus shows you what He wants to give you, be willing to receive it. Ask Him to place what He is giving you in your heart and fill you with the Holy Spirit in any places that are empty. Let Him hug you or hold your hand and give you a physical picture of His love. How does He want to give to you? What does He want to give back to you?

Picture this process with Him and position yourself in a place to receive from Him whatever He wants to give you in a divine exchange.

Ask Him this question: Lord, I have given you all this (rejection, pain, bitterness, control, etc) in the previous session and I have forgiven, now what do You want to give to me in return?

Then write down what He gives to you, speaks to you, and/or shows you. Take time to receive from Him.

{ 6 }

Heart Session: Rewriting Your Story

Rewriting Your Story

YOU CAN KNOW GOD LOVES YOU IN YOUR HEAD, BUT IF YOUR CORE BELIEF SYSTEM SAYS GOD ABANDONED YOU OR OTHERS ABANDONED YOU, THEN IT WILL BE HARD TO EXPERIENCE HIS LOVE.

"Therefore, since we are surrounded by so great a cloud of witnesses [who by faith have testified to the truth of God's absolute faithfulness], stripping off every unnecessary weight and the sin which so easily and cleverly entangles us, let us run with endurance and active persistence the race that is set before us, [looking away from all that will distract us and] focusing our eyes on Jesus, who is the Author and Perfecter of faith [the first incentive for our belief and the One who brings our faith to maturity], who for the joy [of accomplishing the goal] set before Him endured the cross, disregarding the shame, and sat down at the right hand of the throne of God [revealing His deity, His authority, and the completion of His work]." Hebrews 12:1-2 (AMP)

Jesus is the author of our story, and sometimes the weights, sins, and experiences of our lives try to write a different story in our brains. There is a battle that wages in our minds between lies and the truth, and it's up to us to partner with Jesus and change the story. His story is one of redemption, healing, and freedom. His story for us is one of joy and hope. The devil would like to write another story for our lives, and that is the story we need to be sure to tear down. We tear down lies with truth. As we visit the memories and God restores us, we can ask Him to speak truth into the core lies that were created by those experiences. As we break down core lies, we then find ourselves no longer bound to live by them.

Examples of this are core lies of rejection, worthlessness, hopelessness, fear, insecurity, abandonment, abuse. All these things Jesus understands. He faced them all in His humanity, enduring the cross. And because of what He has done through the cross, when we welcome Him in He can rewrite our story!

This starts with inviting Jesus into our lives and making Him Lord, but it doesn't end there. As we continue inviting Him into our hearts and minds, He will rewrite our story with truth. Earlier during the introduction, there was a Scripture from II Corinthians 10:5 that I want to revisit: *"We demolish arguments and every pretension that sets itself up against the knowledge of God, and we take captive every thought to make it obedient to Christ."*

There is an action step we have to take in partnership with what Jesus did on the cross. The action step is to take captive every thought and command it to be obedient to Christ. There is no sin in having a thought that isn't godly. We all have thoughts floating in and out of our mind all day. However, according to Proverbs 23:7, *"as a man thinks in his heart, so is he."* (NKJV) So the thoughts we think are important. When a thought turns into a repeating thought process, that is when we begin to have sin and iniquity and the devil gets a stronghold in our mind and in our heart. This is where our core beliefs start as a child. From our experiences we begin to have thought processes. Some of these thought processes are good. Some of them are not good.

Here are a couple examples of this in real life. A child gets tucked in bed and his mom and dad both tell him every night that they love him, they kiss and hug him, pray for him, and from that some thought processes begin. *I am loved. I am safe. God is real.* Those are some thought processes that will begin to form his core beliefs. Let's say, however, that a child was getting ready for bed, and his dad comes home drunk and yelling at his mom, and he eventually crawls up to bed and tucks himself in, fearful and crying. Core beliefs are forming there too. *I'm alone and unsafe. I'm scared. I have to take care of myself. Men treat women badly. I can't trust people.*

Some of the core beliefs we establish are based in truth and some of them are not. This is why when you know in your head that something is right, it doesn't always connect to your heart. You can know God loves you in your head, but if your core belief system says God abandoned you or others abandoned you, then it will be hard to experience that love.

As we let God rewrite our story, there is nothing He can't do. He created our bodies and He can make new neural pathways for our brain and destroy the old if need be. Often, as people begin to experience God's healing inwardly and allow Him to rewrite their story, we will also see physical healing happen in their body. We are soul, spirit, and body, and every area impacts another. When our soul hurts so can our bodies. People will often experience pain decrease when they forgive. Arthritis disappears as we choose to release offense. God rewrites our story, not just spiritually and emotionally, but often physically as well.

Let's Practice

Read John 8:31-36. Consider the importance of reading and knowing the Word of God in relation to truth and freedom.

Ask the Lord to reveal what core lies you have been believing. As you look at the areas He has healed and touched you as you have worked through this workbook, what lies were there in those situations?

Lord, what lies have I been believing? Lord, would you help me tear down these lies?

After discovering the lies you have been believing, it's important to renounce those lies. You want to tear down any strongholds or core belief systems that were not set up by God. Do this by praying this prayer:

Lord, I renounce the lie (write the specific lie):

You have authority in Jesus, so speak with authority when you say the following statement.

"I come out of agreement with this lie and I command this thought pattern to be broken from my life in Jesus Name."

You may have a few more lies He has shown you. Go ahead and do the same thing with those lies.

Lord, I renounce the lie (write the specific lie):

"I come out of agreement with this lie and I command this thought pattern to be broken from my life in Jesus Name."

Lord, I renounce the lie (write the specific lie):

"I come out of agreement with this lie and I command this thought pattern to be broken from my life in Jesus Name."

Lord, I renounce the lie (write the specific lie):

"I come out of agreement with this lie and I command this thought pattern to be broken from my life in Jesus Name."

Lord, I renounce the lie (write the specific lie):

"I come out of agreement with this lie and I command this thought pattern to be broken from my life in Jesus Name."

Now, ask the Lord to show you what some of the truths have been that He has given you. This is how you give Him permission to rewrite your story.

He may give you a Scripture, or remind you of something that happened during this journey, or maybe give you a brand new truth. His truth will always line up with the Word of God and can be tested in that manner. Also, this isn't always an overnight experience, it may be something that builds in you over time. Just as the lies took time to form, it can take time to renew your heart and mind. It's ok, give yourself grace as you walk it out.

Lord, what truth do you want to speak to me to redeem the lies I have been believing/living in/fighting?

What are the new thought patterns that you want me to form?

What are some Scriptures that would encourage me with establishing this thought pattern?

Lord, would you establish new core belief systems in my life that are full of your truth? I agree with and receive your truth (write truth down):

TRUTH:____

TRUTH:____

TRUTH:____

TRUTH:____

TRUTH:____

TRUTH:____

About the Author
*(Photo credit: Leah Fruth
photography)*

Angela Adkins is a wife, mom, and minister. She loves doing life with her husband and six children. After spending 18 years in Florida, she and her husband Seth Adkins received the call to move to Ohio. She never expected to leave oranges, grapefruit, sunshine, and beaches and trade them for golden retrievers, farm fresh eggs, fog, and snow, but when the Lord says go, it's because He knows best. She and her husband have been in ministry since 2002, and they are presently pastoring a church in Delta, Ohio and helping to develop discipleship groups across Ohio alongside of an awesome team of people.

Angela passionately pursues the Presence of God. She has a desire to see people healed and set free, fully alive in who they are in Christ, and equipped to make a powerful impact on the world around them. She loves to help others discover their gifts and dream big with them.

Resources

If you want further resources and help for healing, freedom, and your relationship with God, check out *angelaadkins.com* and sign up on the email list, read the blog, or schedule an individual heart session in person or through Zoom.

angelaadkins.com

**Photo Credit for cover image goes to Anna Urlapova*